Introduction

This guide is intended to cover the basic steps in collecting good quality herbarium specimens and associated material.

For more information on collecting more specialised plant groups, or more difficult structures, there are a range of more detailed guidelines available online. A list of some of these resources can be found at the end of this guide.

Before collecting any specimens, make sure that you have correct authorisation and permits including local and/or national authority and landowner permission, if required. Any collecting carried out now should be within the terms of the Nagoya Protocol (https://www.cbd.int/abs/). Always be conscious of how much material you take from plants in the wild. While it is preferable to collect sufficient material for duplicate specimens, do not collect at the expense of the wild plants or their habitat.

GH00984722

Field Equipment

Essential equipment for general collecting
clean sharp secateurs & knife
sealable plastic collecting bags in assorted sizes
pencils, permanent pen & ruler
notebook & pre-printed collecting forms
plant press & straps
old newspapers
blotters
jeweller's tags
silica & tea bags
drying equipment/alcohol
hand lens
camera with spare batteries and memory cards
GPS with spare batteries

Additional equipment for specialist groups
cloth seed bags – for fruit, seed, cones etc.
paper packets – for fruit, bryophytes, lichens
waxed paper bags – for fungi
tissue paper – for delicate flowers and fragile fungi
colour chart
hammer and chisel – for lichens
coarse forceps – for algae
muslin/cheesecloth/nappy liners for algae

Desirable equipment
cut-and-hold telescopic pruner
serrated-edge trowel
scalpel
metal, corrugated sheets
laptop

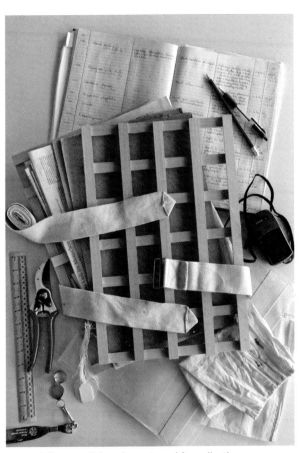

some of the essential equipment used for collecting

Data Collecting

- clear, detailed collecting notes
- clear handwriting – a pencil is best
- consistent information (use a notebook with predefined columns)
- assign a unique running number to each collection
- record the collector's name and number to provide a unique reference for the material
  - record this in the collection notes, on jeweller's tags and newspaper accompanying the specimen and any associated material
  - Use a simple running number for all your collections – all duplicates should receive the same number
- ask local guides for localities

ACE 2	NAME	LOCATION
1	Petrocosmea	Kunming, Western Hills, 2100m
2	Roscoea tibetica	" " 1860m
3	Platycarya strobilacea	" " 1650m
4	Corydalis ? duclouxii	" " 1900m
5	Arisaema ~~erubescens~~ consanguineum Schott	" " 1900m

example of collection notebook

Field notes   Date

Collector   **Collector #**

Plant name

Locality
(including GPS coordinates, latitude and longitude,
national grid reference and altitude)

Habitat
(general surroundings including type of vegetation,
substrate)

Plant description
(as detailed as possible, including characteristics
not captured in the specimen e.g. habit and size;
and those lost on drying e.g. flower colour, smell
and measurements for fleshy material)

Associated material
(material for DNA studies, photo, fruit or seed collected)

Misc.
(any other notes e.g. local names and uses)
N.B. additional date for specialist groups may be required

HABITAT	DESCRIPTION	DATE
Limestone, E-facing crevice	Grey-green rosette; fls blue-mauve with white throat + two dark spots	7.6.94
Open pine forest glade	lvs 1-3. fls purple with faint white lines	''
Open limestone hillside	Much-branched small tree to 5m. fls ♀ & ♂ pale green	''
Limestone rocks & crevices	Fibrous rooted; lvs grey-green, paler beneath. fls pinky-purple, darker at tip of petals.	''
Limestone rock pockets	30-45 cm. lvs mid-green, slight pink flush along mid-rib. Spathe pale green below, purple brown at top + appendage.	''

Collecting Plant Material

- assign a unique running number to the collection and write it on the newspaper and a jeweller's tag
- select material from the plant
  - for larger plants take all material from a single individual – do not mix individuals
  - for smaller plants, where multiple individuals are collected, any associated material must be linked to the correct individual
  - include both flowers and fruit if possible
  - include extra leaf, flower and fruit material for later dissection
  - include roots, bulbs or corms if possible

collecting plant material using a cut-and-hold telescopic pruner

top and bottom: selecting material to collect

7

Preparing Material for Pressing

- remove soil

- remove any obvious insects

- ensure material will fit a standard herbarium sheet (42 x 26.4 cm). Either trim excess or divide into two or more sheets, clearly marked as such (sheet 1 of 2, sheet 2 of 2)

- remove any excess material to reduce bulkiness and ensure important features are visible

- make all cuts obvious e.g. keep leaf base or section of petiole on specimen

- prepare a flower to show internal structure

- cut fruits and seeds, fleshy roots/bulbs/corms in half

- any bulky fruits or seeds need a separate label

preparing material for pressing

trimming to fit sheet

flower dissection

fruit dissection

Pressing Plant Material

- lay out on a folded sheet of newspaper
  - leave space for label and a capsule (envelope) to contain loose material
  - leave loose – do not attach to newspaper with tape

- mark newspaper with name and collection number on outside bottom left hand corner – clearly mark any specimens which need more than one sheet

- ensure that both sides of the leaf can be seen by turning at least one leaf the other way up. If there is only one leaf fold it to show both sides

- fold any long stems or leaves into 'N' 'V' or 'Z' shapes as appropriate

- place newspaper between blotting paper in a plant press
  - if you don't have a plant press, use pieces of corrugated cardboard cut out of a large box and two metal baking/cooking grid cooling racks

specimen cut to size and arranged to show characters

specimen in newspaper between blotters in plant press

specimen showing both sides of leaf, cuts made obvious and 'N' shape fold used

Drying

- drying

  - dry specimens using a drying frame over a source of heat

  - ensure the heat source is not too hot, to prevent the specimens becoming brittle

  - alternatively place the plant press in a warm, dry place

  - keep the number of specimens in the press to a minimum to aid drying

  - change the blotting paper daily until the specimens are dry

  - corrugated metal sheets can be used at intervals in the press to increase heat and air flow

- the alcohol (Schweinfurth) method

  - if it is not possible to dry the specimens in the field then 60-80% alcohol can be used to maintain the specimens until they can be dried

  - do not use blotters or corrugate

  - take a stack of specimens in newspapers, compress and tie them and place the stack into a heavy-duty plastic bag

  - for each 12–15 cm stack of specimens, sprinkle 0.5 l alcohol into the bag and then seal the bag using tape

  - the alcohol vaporises in the bag and will keep the specimens for several weeks if the bag is not punctured

N.B. using alcohol denatures DNA and specimens will discolour

preparing the press for drying

drying frame with gas stove before cover attached

drying frame with electric heaters and cover

drying specimens in the sun

Fruit and seeds

- bulky fruits or seeds will need to be dried separately outside the plant press
- they can be placed inside an envelope made from newspaper or cloth bag and laid out in a warm, dry place
- they will need a separate jeweller's tag which should have the same number as the associated pressed specimen

cloth bags and botanical envelopes for collecting seed and fruits

Collecting into Spirit

For certain groups and for particular research, some flowering and fruiting material is best collected into liquid to preserve its three-dimensional structure. This is commonly done for plants in families with zygomorphic flowers, such as Gesneriaceae, Orchidaceae and Zingiberaceae.

- collect into bottles/jars containing 70% alcohol (ethanol) to cover the material. Fill the bottle completely because a bubble of air will damage the material as it is carried in the field

- material may include an entire inflorescence, or several single flowers with their subtending bracts and bracteoles if present

  - for Zingiberaceae, prepare a longitudinal half or quarter of large inflorescences or infructescences, or several bracts with complete cincinni

- the collection number should be written on thick archival paper using a dark pencil and placed inside the bottle/jar

- for permanent preservation the material should be transferred to Copenhagen Solution (70% industrial methylated spirit, 28% distilled water and 2% glycerol)

Collecting Material for DNA

- select youngish leaves or flower buds with no visible dirt, fungus or other damage (avoid very young or old leaves)

- collect at least 5 cm of leaf material

- tear larger leaves into approximately 1 cm sections, a large midrib can be discarded

- write the same collection number as the herbarium specimen on a teabag

- place leaf fragments into the teabag along with a jeweller's tag bearing the collection number

- place the teabag into a container of silica gel as quickly as possible after collecting the material

- ensure that the teabag has full contact with the silica gel to dry the material as rapidly as possible

selecting leaf material, tearing up leaf material and removing midrib, teabag containing 1 cm sections of leaf and jeweller's tag, placing teabag into container of silica gel

Labels & Capsules

- print labels on archive-quality paper (acid-free)
- trim excess white space from label
- there should be a label for each duplicate
- if specimens require more than one sheet, each sheet should have a label
- any additional material, such as carpological, spirit or silica-dried material, should also have a label
- place at least one leaf, or part of a leaf, as well as at least one flower or fruit for anatomical work, in an archive-quality capsule (envelope) for dissection

---

Royal Botanic Garden Edinburgh
FLORA OF SCOTLAND

Ligusticum scoticum **L.**

Locality: UNITED KINGDOM: Scotland: (VC 111) Orkney: Mainland, Kirkwall; just before Churchill Barrier No 1. Rocky coastal slopes with *Honkenya peploides*. 5 m. 58°53'50"N, 2°54'00"W. Locally abundant.

Notes: Perennial to 60 cm tall.

Collectors: Gardner, Martin Fraser & Knees, Sabina Georgina

Coll.Num.: 8545

Date: 4 Jul 2009

---

example of herbarium specimen label

example of herbarium specimen label

Collecting Bryophytes and Lichens

- use paper packets or bags (or envelopes or newspaper, sealed at one end) to collect lichens and bryophytes

- sporophytes should be included in bryophyte collections wherever possible, and dioicous species both male and female plants where possible

- the entire thallus should be included for lichens, or at least connections to substrate and growing edges

- packets should be clearly labelled with collector and collection number

- specimens should be air dried at ambient temperature as quickly as possible to prevent mould
    - ideally open the packets/bags
    - use a fan to provide air circulation
    - avoid direct heat

- after drying, transfer specimens to archival paper storage packets
    - ensure all material, including any dirt at the bottom, is transferred, as this may include small structures that have become detached

- in addition to the standard collection information, also record:
    - substrate, and microhabitat (e.g. dry side of tree; moist horizontal branch; base-rich rocks beside stream)

bryophyte specimens drying with cool fans

Collecting Fungi

- waxed paper is best for collecting fungi – either as sandwich bags or cut from a baking roll
- avoid collecting with fingers only, instead cut, or dig up, specimens and take care not to over-handle them, which causes loss of important characters (e.g. tiny hairs on stipe)
- place the wrapped specimens in an open basket
  - do not press fungi specimens flat; collect all growth stages possible from young to old
- care must be taken to record details of the fungal fruiting body prior to drying
- if possible make a spore print with a mature cap
- fungi specimens need to be dried as soon as possible using one of the following techniques:
  - a food dehydrator with the temperature set between 42^{0}C and 55^{0}C
  - air dry with a heat source e.g. table lamp, sunny spot or rack above a radiator
- in addition to the standard collection information, also record:
  - substrate – essential information includes whether you are under hardwoods or conifers and whether the fruiting body was growing from wood or an underground root
  - associated plants/trees
  - colours, textures and patterning of all parts (cap, stipe, gills, oxidation reactions of cap and stipe) using a standard colour chart
  - smell
  - presence and staining of latex if present
  - presence of droplets or veil fragments below cap or on stipe

Collecting Ferns

- always collect fertile material, dimorphic fronds (where present), stipe bases and rhizomes

- for small species collect whole plants and a sample of a larger population

- for large ferns keep:
    - the tip of the frond, a middle or largest pinna and a basal or smallest pinna
    - rhizome and stipe can be tagged separately if too large/bulky for a herbarium sheet

- ensure the lower lamina, sori, stipe bases and rhizomes that clearly display scales and hairs (if present) are visible when mounted

- to fit a large fern to a herbarium sheet either:
    - fold over the top half of the frond to show the opposite side to the base
    - turn over a pinna or two to show sori

- in addition to the standard collection information, also record:
    - the width of the frond and the length of the stipe
    - if the basal pinna bears pinnae
    - rhizome branching pattern
    - overall frond shape
    - the internal structure of stipe bases and rhizomes

Collecting Aquatic Plants

- keep specimens in a bag or bucket of water until ready to press

- very small plants, e.g. duckweed, are best collected in a small bottle with water and later transferred into a solution to preserve them

- plants that are emergent, and those that don't clump when taken from water, can be pressed using standard techniques

- plants that clump and are not rigid, or those that become flaccid when removed from water, need to be floated onto card

    - arrange plant from root end as card is slowly removed from water

    - drain as much water as possible from card

    - once mounted place blotting paper over the specimen to aid drying, then place card and blotter in a newspaper folder and follow standard procedure

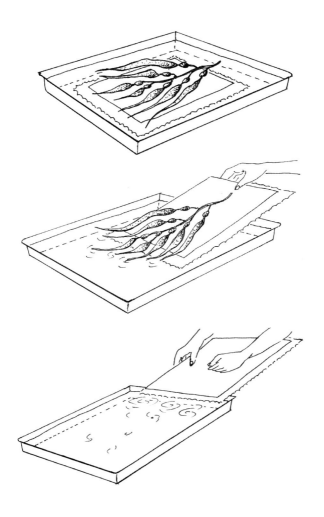

floating aquatic plants/algae onto card

Collecting Algae

- a knife or coarse forceps may be required to remove some specimens from the rock surface

- larger, thicker specimens may be best fixed with ca. 4% formaldehyde prior to pressing
  - if first fixed with formaldehyde, the alga can be rinsed free of preservative and then pressed
  - alternatively the alga could be transferred to Copenhagen Solution (see Collecting in Spirit)

- to press:
  - robust specimens may be placed directly onto paper; more delicate specimens need to be floated onto card in water
  - have a shallow tray which is larger than the paper and add sufficient seawater to cover the card and specimen
  - a firm metal or plastic mesh may be used to support the card
  - float the specimen onto the card and arrange it to show the shape and branching pattern of the alga – a paintbrush, forceps, etc. may be used to arrange the specimen
  - once arranged, the card should be withdrawn carefully from the water, at an angle to allow excess water to drain
  - place muslin (cheesecloth, nappy liners or similar alternatives) on top of the specimen and then blotting material (blotting paper, newspaper) to soak up moisture

- in addition to the standard collection information, also record:
  - location on shore, depth and whether it is a cast alga, etc.

Submitting Specimens to a Herbarium

This is a checklist to use if you intend to submit your specimens to a herbarium:

- ❏ separate duplicates for distribution and submit one specimen to each institute

- ❏ check specimens will fit a standard herbarium sheet 42 cm x 26.4 cm

- ❏ prepare a capsule with dissection material

- ❏ check large specimens to be mounted on two or more sheets are clearly marked sheet 1 of 2 etc.

- ❏ check each specimen has a label

- ❏ check associated material has labels

- ❏ if you are creating the labels by electronic means please give an electronic copy of the data to the herbarium at the same time as submitting the specimens

- ❏ it is **essential** that you submit your collecting permit along with the specimens in accordance with the Nagoya Protocol

References & Resources

Videos

- RBGE Herbarium: Basic Plant Collecting and Pressing video:
  http://bit.ly/2ozXWnG
- RBGE Specimen Mounting video:
  http://bit.ly/2qaamQi

Online resources

- Collecting and preserving plant specimens, a manual (Queensland, 2016):
  https://www.qld.gov.au/environment/assets/documents/plants-animals/herbarium/collecting-manual.pdf
- Field Techniques Used by Missouri Botanical Garden:
  http://www.mobot.org/MOBOT/molib/fieldtechbook/welcome.shtml
- A guide to collecting herbarium specimens of ferns and their allies:
  http://www.anbg.gov.au/fern/collecting.html
- Collecting specimens (The British Lichen Society):
  http://www.britishlichensociety.org.uk/identification/collecting-specimens
- Collecting and recording fungi (British Mycological Society):
  www.britmycolsoc.org.uk/index.php/download_file/view/221/
- Collecting and pressing specimens (Botanical Society of Britain and Ireland):
  http://bsbi.org.uk/Collecting.pdf
- Collecting and Preserving Aquatic Plants (Warrington, P., 1994):
  www.env.gov.bc.ca/wat/wq/plants/plantcollect.pdf
- Vanderpoorten, A., Papp, B. & Gradstein, R. (2010) Chapter 13 - Sampling of Bryophytes. Abc Taxa. 8: 331-345:
  http://www.abctaxa.be/volumes/volume-8-manual-atbi/

Literature

- Wilkie, P, Poulsen, AD, Harris, D & Forrest, LL (2013). 'The collection and storage of plant material for DNA extraction: The Teabag Method', The Gardens' Bulletin Singapore, 65(2): 231-234
- Bridson, D & Forman, L (2010) The Herbarium Handbook Kew Publishing.